EXECUTION EXCELLENCE

How to Beat Procrastination and Achieve Your Goals

ALEXIS KING

TABLE OF CONTENTS

UNDERSTANDING PROCRASTINATION

· ★ ·

Procrastination is something everyone faces at some point in life. But why do we procrastinate? Is it merely about putting off tasks, or does it run deeper?

Delaying important responsibilities often leads to stress and frustration, but to truly understand procrastination, we need to look at the reasons behind it. It's not just about avoiding work—there are often psychological reasons at play.

So, how can understanding these reasons help us recognize our habits and take steps toward overcoming them?

When you hear the word "procrastination," do you immediately picture someone idling away time? It might surprise you to learn that procrastination comes in different forms. Typically, it falls into two categories: active and passive procrastination.

Have you ever found yourself delaying an important task but still keeping busy? That's active procrastination. For instance, a student might avoid writing a paper by choosing to clean their room instead. It seems productive, but is it really just an excuse to dodge the main task?

Some studies even question whether active procrastinators are truly procrastinating since they are, after all, completing other tasks.

Now, let's consider passive procrastination. Unlike active procrastinators, passive procrastinators don't switch to other tasks. They freeze, often overwhelmed by indecision. Have you ever been in a situation where you're paralyzed by the thought of starting a daunting task? As the deadline inches closer, stress rises, leading to a cycle of avoidance. This form of procrastination can take a serious toll, not only on productivity but also on emotional well-being.

Procrastination can show up in various areas of life. Recognizing these patterns helps highlight its impact. For example, have you noticed how common procrastination is among students? Academic procrastination—delaying studying until the last minute—leads to poor performance and unnecessary stress. In the workplace, employees might put off essential tasks, like preparing for a big presentation, which can jeopardize their success. Even in daily life, people procrastinate, whether it's ignoring chores or postponing health appointments. Understanding how procrastination infiltrates different areas can help us see its wide-reaching effects.

The consequences of procrastination can be quite damaging. Passive procrastinators, in particular, experience the snowball effect of inaction. Does the stress of putting off tasks ever make you feel trapped, lowering your self-esteem? This gap between your aspirations and your actions can be frustrating. Acknowledging that procrastination hinders personal growth might just be the motivation needed to stop procrastinating and embrace more proactive habits.

What about active procrastinators? They might believe that working under pressure enhances their performance. Do you think you work better at the last minute? While this may sometimes feel true, it's a risky strategy. Over time, this pattern can lead to burnout. Meeting deadlines is one thing, but how often does the quality of work suffer when it's done in a rush? By reevaluating the effects of active procrastination, individuals can assess whether their approach truly supports their goals.

So, how can you stop procrastinating and become more productive? One effective way is to set clear, achievable goals. Have you ever felt overwhelmed by a large task? Breaking it down into smaller steps makes it feel more manageable. Establishing mini-deadlines for these steps creates a sense of urgency and helps maintain motivation. Could an accountability partner help keep you on track? Sometimes, external encouragement is just the push needed to prevent procrastination.

Another powerful strategy for stopping procrastination is self-awareness. Are there specific moments when you're more likely to procrastinate? Recognizing these triggers gives you the chance to pause and reassess. What's really holding you back? Creating a daily routine that balances work and breaks can help minimize procrastination. Prioritizing tasks early in the day, when you're most focused, might be key to staying productive.

By taking proactive steps, you can stop procrastinating and begin to enjoy a more productive and less stressful approach to your tasks.

PSYCHOLOGICAL REASONS BEHIND PROCRASTINATION

———————— • ★ • ————————

Understanding the psychological aspects of procrastination is key to gaining self-awareness and improving productivity. One major factor? The fear of failure. Have you ever avoided a task because you were worried you wouldn't meet expectations? This fear can serve as a defense mechanism, preventing you from even starting. Think about a time when you delayed beginning a work project because you were afraid it wouldn't turn out well. Acknowledging this fear is the first step toward loosening its grip and pushing yourself to take action.

Another significant factor contributing to procrastination is perfectionism. Do you ever find yourself waiting for the "perfect moment" to start something? Striving for perfection can create intense pressure, leading to delays. Many people hold off on tasks until they believe everything is just right, which often results in missed deadlines. If you recognize this pattern in yourself, ask: are your standards realistic? Focusing on progress, rather than perfection, can help you avoid the pitfalls of procrastination caused by high expectations.

But what if the real issue is a lack of motivation? This often happens when tasks feel unimportant or unclear. When a project doesn't seem personally valuable, isn't it tempting to keep putting it off? One way to combat this is by redefining your goals and ensuring they align with your personal interests. Have you ever found that breaking a big task into smaller, more manageable steps makes it feel less daunting? Connecting each step to a larger objective can help reignite your motivation and keep procrastination at bay.

Self-efficacy—the belief in your ability to succeed—also plays a crucial role in procrastination. Do you ever doubt your capacity to tackle difficult tasks? People who lack confidence in their abilities are more likely to procrastinate, avoiding challenges altogether. Building self-efficacy, however, can counter this tendency. Have you noticed how small successes can boost your confidence? Achievements, no matter how minor, reinforce your belief in yourself and make it easier to face bigger tasks without hesitation.

Let's consider some examples to see how these factors play out in real life. Imagine a writer who avoids starting an article because they worry about how others will judge it. By reflecting on this fear and accepting that the first draft doesn't need to be perfect, they can ease into the writing process. Similarly, think about an entrepreneur who delays launching a product because they want it to be flawless. Wouldn't it be more productive to launch and then adapt based on customer feedback? Realizing that nothing can be perfect the first time can empower individuals to move forward and make necessary improvements along the way.

Motivation is another critical element. Have you ever struggled with a task that felt disconnected from your personal goals? Breaking the task into smaller, more manageable pieces can create a sense of immediate satisfaction, making it easier to get started. Establishing a clear purpose for each task also makes it more appealing. When your work connects to something meaningful, doesn't diving in become much easier?

By understanding these psychological factors, you can stop procrastinating and create strategies to overcome these common barriers.

COMMON PROCRASTINATION TRIGGERS

———————— • ★ • ————————

Recognizing the specific triggers of procrastination is essential for overcoming it. Have you ever wondered why distractions—both external and internal—play such a big role in delaying tasks? In today's digital age, it's hard to stay focused when phone notifications and social media constantly pull for our attention. Do you find that even a quick glance at a notification can completely derail your focus? Internal distractions, such as wandering thoughts, can be just as disruptive. How can you manage these distractions? Practicing mindfulness, such as setting specific times to check messages and focusing on your breathing, can help keep distractions at bay.

Another common trigger is feeling overwhelmed. Have you ever faced a task so large that you didn't know where to begin? This sense of being overwhelmed can cause you to freeze. The solution? Break big tasks down into smaller, more manageable steps. Does outlining actionable steps make the process seem less intimidating? By focusing on each small step, progress feels more achievable, and the task becomes less daunting.

Social pressures can also contribute to procrastination. Have you ever noticed how the attitudes of those around you affect your work habits? In some environments, procrastination is normalized, and it's easy to fall into the same patterns. How can you avoid this? Surrounding yourself with people who excel in time management can influence your own productivity. Being open about deadlines and setting collective goals with colleagues can align social interactions with a more productive mindset.

Another significant trigger is the lack of accountability. Without deadlines or oversight, how easy is it to keep pushing tasks off? Setting regular check-ins with a colleague or manager can create the sense of obligation that leads to timely completion. Have you ever tried using task management apps or setting personal deadlines? These tools add layers of commitment, making it harder to procrastinate.

Key Things To Note

By exploring the roots and triggers of procrastination, you gain valuable insights into your behaviors. Have you considered how understanding the different types of procrastination can provide clarity on why you delay tasks? Recognizing procrastination's impact on both your personal and professional life allows you to make conscious efforts to change your habits. Implementing effective strategies and acknowledging psychological factors gives you the power to stop procrastinating and make meaningful progress. Through these approaches, you can improve productivity and work more efficiently toward your goals.

References

Active and Passive Procrastination: Definitions, Examples, Differences, and Criticisms – Solving Procrastination. (n.d.).
https://solvingprocrastination.com/active-passive-procrastination/

Sirois, F. M. (2023, March 13). Procrastination and Stress: A Conceptual Review of Why Context Matters. International Journal of

Environmental Research and Public Health.
https://doi.org/10.3390/ijerph20065031

Shatz, I. (2019). Why people procrastinate: The psychology and causes of procrastination – Solving Procrastination. Solvingprocrastination.com. https://solvingprocrastination.com/why-people-procrastinate/

Voge, D. (2007). Understanding and Overcoming Procrastination. McGraw Center for Teaching and Learning; Princeton University. https://mcgraw.princeton.edu/undergraduates/resources/resource-library/understanding-and-overcoming-procrastination

Yan, B., & Zhang, X. (2022, February 2). What Research Has Been Conducted on Procrastination? Evidence From a Systematical Bibliometric Analysis. Frontiers in Psychology. https://doi.org/10.3389/fpsyg.2022.809044

Zohar, A. H., Shimone, L. P., & Hen, M. (2019, May 29). Active and passive procrastination in terms of temperament and character. PeerJ. https://doi.org/10.7717/peerj.6988

IDENTIFYING YOUR PROCRASTINATION PATTERNS

* ★ *

Have you ever wondered why you keep putting off tasks, even when you know they're important? Understanding your procrastination patterns is key to improving both work performance and personal productivity. But where do these tendencies come from? This chapter dives into the habits and triggers that lead to procrastination, helping you recognize your own behaviors. Once you can identify these patterns, doesn't it become easier to address them head-on?

Common emotional responses like anxiety or perfectionism often play a significant role. Do you find yourself avoiding tasks because you're afraid they won't be good enough? Perfectionism can paralyze progress, leaving you stuck in a cycle of delay. On the other hand, environmental factors, such as a cluttered workspace or constant interruptions, can make focusing on tasks feel impossible. Have you ever tried working in a messy space and noticed how much harder it is to concentrate? Spotting these distractions is the first step in tackling them effectively.

Why is it so important to recognize these triggers? By becoming more aware of what's holding you back, you can develop targeted strategies to stop procrastinating and start making progress. Whether it's reorganizing your workspace or addressing the underlying emotions, this chapter will guide you toward greater self-awareness and, ultimately, more productive habits.

SELF-ASSESSMENT TECHNIQUES

———————— ⋆ ★ ⋆ ————————

Understanding your procrastination habits is essential for improving work performance and personal productivity. But how do you get started? Recognizing your patterns requires practical, actionable methods. This chapter explores various self-assessment tools that can help you evaluate your procrastination behaviors and highlight areas for improvement. Ready to dive in?

Write it Down (or Use Notes in Your Phone)

Have you ever thought about tracking your procrastination habits? Keeping a daily list of tasks and moments when procrastination occurs can be a game-changer. Writing down which tasks you avoided, why you delayed them, and what you did instead can reveal surprising patterns. For example, do you often avoid starting reports? By journaling, you may discover that the root cause is a fear of failure or simply a lack of interest. Reflecting on these entries makes procrastination feel more tangible, giving you the chance to address it directly.

To make the most of this technique, build a routine of logging your tasks and instances of procrastination consistently. What details should you capture? Pay attention to timing, context, and emotions tied to procrastination episodes. Over time, reviewing these notes can highlight recurring triggers, helping you take concrete steps toward improvement.

Reflection Questions

Sometimes, the reasons behind procrastination run deeper. How can you uncover these hidden behaviors? Using reflection questions can enhance your self-awareness and accountability. Ask yourself questions like, "What emotions do I feel when I think about this task?" or "Why am I delaying this project?" These questions prompt introspection, helping you identify negative thought patterns or anxieties that might be fueling your procrastination.

If you often postpone tasks requiring focus, ask yourself, "Do I find this task overwhelming or beyond my abilities?" Uncovering this self-doubt could lead you to break the task into smaller, more manageable steps or seek help when needed. Reflection questions serve as a diagnostic tool, clarifying which areas need attention and offering a roadmap for change.

Surveys and Quizzes

What about taking a more objective approach? Using validated self-assessment tools like the General Procrastination Scale or the Tuckman Procrastination Scale can provide an external perspective on your procrastination tendencies. Have you ever tried comparing your habits with broader data? These surveys measure procrastination across various contexts—work, study, or personal projects—offering valuable insights into your behaviors.

Taking these surveys periodically can track your progress. If you score high on impulsiveness-related questions, for example, this might signal the need to improve impulse control techniques. Could setting stricter schedules or reducing distractions be the solution? Using these structured tools gives you a measurable way to understand and tackle procrastination.

Peer Feedback

Sometimes, the people around us can spot procrastination patterns we're unaware of. Have you considered asking trusted friends or colleagues for feedback? Their observations might uncover habits you hadn't noticed. For instance, a colleague may point out that while you tend to delay starting projects, you perform exceptionally well under pressure. Could this indicate a preference for working under tight deadlines?

When seeking peer feedback, it's important to ask the right questions. What procrastination habits have they noticed? How do they view your overall productivity? By opening yourself to their insights, you gain a new perspective that complements your self-assessments. Integrating both external feedback and personal reflections creates a fuller understanding of your procrastination tendencies.

Final Thoughts

By applying these self-assessment techniques—journaling, reflection questions, surveys, and peer feedback—you can systematically evaluate your procrastination habits. Each method offers unique insights, helping you stop procrastinating and boost your productivity. Whether it's tracking your behavior through journaling or using surveys for objective data, these strategies provide a comprehensive approach to overcoming procrastination.

UNDERSTANDING PERSONAL PROCRASTINATION TRIGGERS

— • ★ • —

To effectively manage procrastination, have you ever considered what specifically triggers it for you? Recognizing these triggers is crucial for overcoming them. Often, emotional triggers play a significant role in delaying tasks.

Does anxiety, fear of failure, or perfectionism make certain tasks feel unbearable? These emotions can cause you to seek the immediate relief of avoiding the task altogether. But how can you counteract these feelings?

The first step is identifying and understanding these emotional triggers. Have you tried journaling your reactions to tasks? For instance, if you notice increased anxiety when a big project deadline looms, breaking that project into smaller, more manageable tasks could be the key. Seeking help from coworkers or practicing mindfulness techniques might also help in managing stress and reducing procrastination.

Environmental triggers are just as important in influencing procrastination. Have you ever felt overwhelmed by your workspace? A cluttered, noisy, or chaotic environment can seriously affect your ability to focus. What if you organized your workspace to make it more conducive to productivity? A clean and decluttered environment makes it easier to start working. Investing in noise-canceling headphones can help reduce distractions, and setting clear boundaries with people around you during work hours can minimize interruptions. Doesn't creating a focus-friendly environment make procrastination less likely?

Task-related triggers are another common cause of procrastination. Do you tend to delay tasks that feel complex or difficult? This hesitation might arise from unclear instructions, insufficient resources, or simply the overwhelming size of the task. How can you overcome this? One effective strategy is to break the task down into smaller steps. Wouldn't a clear roadmap make it feel less intimidating? Asking for help or ensuring you have the right resources can make the task more achievable. Simplifying the process reduces the resistance you might feel toward starting and completing it.

Finally, time-related triggers play a huge role in procrastination. Poor time management and unrealistic expectations can create a stressful environment that makes it easy to procrastinate. Have you ever thought about how your perception of time affects your work habits? Aligning tasks with your peak productivity times could lead to better results. If you're most productive in the morning, doesn't it make sense to schedule your most demanding tasks for that time? Time management techniques like the Pomodoro Technique—working in focused intervals followed by breaks—can also help improve productivity and minimize burnout.

TRACKING AND ANALYZING PROCRASTINATION INSTANCES

———— • ★ • ————

Encouraging readers to track procrastination can significantly improve their ability to understand and manage it. Have you ever kept a detailed record of your procrastination? When analyzed thoughtfully, this practice helps identify patterns of avoidance and blockages in productivity, ultimately improving time management and efficiency.

Maintaining daily logs is a powerful tool in this exploration. What if you consistently noted which tasks you completed and which you postponed? By recording reasons for delays, emotions you experienced, and external factors that played a role, you can start to see patterns emerge. If anxiety or disinterest are common reasons for procrastination, wouldn't recognizing these emotions help you confront them more effectively? Over time, these records give a holistic view of your habits, making it easier to adjust procrastination tendencies.

One effective technique for analyzing this data is combining frequency analysis and root cause analysis. Frequency analysis reveals how often procrastination occurs, while root cause analysis helps you understand why it happens. Have you ever thought about using visual data to simplify this process? Charts and graphs can clarify patterns, making it easier to draw actionable insights. For instance, if you notice that you tend to procrastinate on specific tasks—like paperwork or creative writing—doesn't that give you the information you need to create targeted strategies for managing those challenges? Visual aids, such as pie charts, can highlight areas that need the most attention.

Timing analysis takes this one step further by examining when procrastination happens during the day. Have you ever noticed that your productivity varies based on the time of day? Many people find that their energy levels fluctuate, affecting when they are most productive. By tracking when tasks are delayed versus when they're completed, you can pinpoint your most productive times. If you discover that you work best in the mornings but often procrastinate in the afternoons, wouldn't it make sense to schedule your most challenging tasks for the morning and save lighter work for later? Aligning your tasks with your energy levels can greatly improve efficiency.

Regular reflection is key to making the most of your data. Do you set aside time to review your logs? Reflecting on your findings weekly or monthly allows you to spot trends and make necessary adjustments. Asking yourself questions like, "What were my main distractions this week?" or "How did my emotions impact my work?" can reveal deeper insights into your procrastination patterns. This type of self-assessment promotes a growth mindset, encouraging ongoing progress.

Insights and Implications

Recognizing and addressing procrastination is crucial for boosting productivity and achieving career goals. This chapter emphasizes the importance of self-assessment tools in identifying procrastination habits. Have you tried methods like journaling, reflective questioning, or using validated surveys? These tools not only help you recognize patterns of behavior but also empower you to develop concrete strategies to manage them.

Incorporating these techniques into your daily routine builds accountability and self-awareness. Once you understand the specific triggers of your procrastination—whether they are emotional, environmental, task-related, or time-based—doesn't it become easier to create tailored solutions? Regularly tracking and analyzing instances of procrastination provides valuable insights that support continuous improvement, ensuring both personal and professional growth. This holistic approach leads to enhanced performance and satisfaction, both at work and in life.

References

Hensley, L. C., & Munn, K. J. (2020). The power of writing about procrastination: journaling as a tool for change. Journal of Further and Higher Education, 44(1), 16-27. https://doi.org/10.1080/0309877X.2019.1702154

Kagan, J. (2022, October 3). Time Logs: What are they? And Why are They Important? Niftypm.com. https://niftypm.com/blog/time-logs/

Lieberman, C. (2019, March 25). Why You Procrastinate (It Has Nothing to Do With Self-Control). The New York Times. https://www.nytimes.com/2019/03/25/smarter-living/why-you-procrastinate-it-has-nothing-to-do-with-self-control.html

Sirois, F. M. (2023, March 13). Procrastination and Stress: A Conceptual Review of Why Context Matters. International Journal of Environmental Research and Public Health. https://doi.org/10.3390/ijerph20065031

Team EmpMonitor. (2024, April 16). Daily Activity Log: 5 Tips On Enhancing Productivity. Blog | Employee Management System | EmpMonitor. https://empmonitor.com/blog/daily-activity-log-tips/

Yan, B., & Zhang, X. (2022, February 2). What Research Has Been Conducted on Procrastination? Evidence From a Systematical

Bibliometric Analysis. Frontiers in Psychology. https://doi.org/10.3389/fpsyg.2022.809044

OVERCOMING PROCRASTINATION: TOOLS AND TECHNIQUES

———————— • ★ • ————————

Overcoming procrastination isn't just about finding the motivation to get things done; it's about understanding why we delay tasks and using effective tools to stop this habit. By addressing both the mental and practical sides of procrastination, professionals can learn to manage their time better and work toward their goals. This chapter offers a range of tools and techniques designed to help readers combat procrastination and boost productivity.

We'll explore practical methods like breaking tasks into smaller parts, the 2-Minute Rule, and task segmentation. Have you ever considered using bullet journals or lists to track your progress? We'll also cover the importance of setting realistic deadlines, incorporating buffer time, and making public commitments to stay accountable. By the end of this chapter, you'll have a toolkit of strategies that can help you stop procrastinating and keep moving forward in both your professional and personal life.

Breaking Tasks into Manageable Chunks

One of the most effective ways to overcome procrastination is to break larger tasks into smaller, more manageable chunks. Does tackling a big project feel overwhelming? By dividing it into smaller, bite-sized pieces, you can make progress consistently without feeling daunted. Let's explore a few strategies that can help break down your workload.

The 2-Minute Rule, introduced by productivity expert David Allen, is a powerful way to start. This rule states that if a task can be completed in two minutes or less, you should do it immediately. Doesn't it feel great to get small tasks out of the way? Whether it's responding to an email, tidying your workspace, or sorting a document, handling these tasks right away reduces mental clutter and builds momentum for larger projects. It's a simple way to clear your mind and set the stage for tackling more significant challenges.

Task segmentation is another key technique. This method involves breaking a large project into smaller, actionable steps. Have you ever noticed how much easier it is to focus when you have a clear plan? For instance, writing a report can be segmented into research, outlining, drafting, and revising. Each step becomes a mini-task, bringing a sense of accomplishment and keeping you on track without getting overwhelmed by the big picture.

Using tools like bullet journals or task lists is also incredibly effective. Have you tried visually laying out your tasks? Bullet journaling combines to-do lists, calendars, and notes into one system, helping you see what needs to be done and prioritize your workload. Checking off completed tasks gives you a sense of progress, which keeps you motivated. Creating daily or weekly lists can help you stay focused on your immediate tasks while keeping long-term goals in sight.

Setting Realistic Deadlines and Time Limits

Setting realistic deadlines, along with time limits for specific tasks, creates urgency and prevents procrastination. Have you ever noticed how giving yourself a set amount of time to complete something pushes you to act quickly? One useful method is the Pomodoro Technique, which involves working for 25 minutes on a task followed by a short break. This structured approach helps maintain productivity without leading to burnout.

By setting specific timeframes for each segment of work, you encourage yourself to act quickly, reducing the likelihood that tasks will be delayed indefinitely. Whether it's the Pomodoro Technique or simply setting a deadline for each part of a larger project, these techniques help you maintain a sense of progress and discipline throughout the day.

Accountability and Review

Making public commitments and regularly reviewing your deadlines can also keep you on track. Have you ever told someone about your goals? Sharing your deadlines with others creates accountability, making it harder to procrastinate. Regularly reviewing your progress and deadlines allows you to make necessary adjustments and stay focused on your goals.

However, it's important to assess how well these techniques are working for you. Have you found that certain methods work better than others? What might work for one person may not work for another, so flexibility is key. By taking time to review and adapt your approach, you can ensure your strategy fits your needs and aligns with your goals.

Setting Realistic Deadlines

Establishing realistic deadlines is essential for maintaining accountability and combating procrastination. Deadlines provide structure, helping you focus on tasks and manage your time more effectively. Without clear deadlines, tasks can seem overwhelming and vague, which often leads to procrastination. This section will explain why setting achievable deadlines is crucial and how to do it effectively.

One proven method for setting clear deadlines is by using the SMART criteria. Have you heard of this approach? SMART stands for Specific, Measurable, Achievable, Relevant, and Time-bound. By following these guidelines, your goals become clearer and easier to achieve within a specific timeframe. Instead of saying, "finish the report soon," try "complete the 20-page marketing report by next Friday." Wouldn't that make the task feel more manageable? Having a clear target reduces the chances of feeling overwhelmed, helping you avoid procrastination.

Another important aspect of setting deadlines is incorporating buffer time. Have you ever been blindsided by an unexpected issue that threw off your schedule? Buffer time helps to account for those moments. Whether it's a surprise meeting or a personal obligation, adding extra time to your deadlines can reduce stress and improve the quality of your work. For example, if a project is due in two weeks, planning to finish it in ten days gives you room for last-minute surprises. Isn't it better to be prepared for the unexpected?

Making public commitments is another powerful tool for enhancing accountability. Have you ever told someone else about your goals? When you share your deadlines with peers or mentors, you create a social contract that increases the likelihood of meeting your timeline. If others know about your goals, you might feel an extra sense of motivation to achieve them. For example, a writer might tell their writing group, "I plan to finish the first draft of my novel by the end of the month." Does the added pressure of public commitment make it easier to stay on track?

It's also important to regularly review your deadlines to maintain flexibility. Life can be unpredictable, and priorities can shift quickly. Taking time to evaluate your timelines and make necessary adjustments keeps your workflow adaptable. For instance, a manager might review their team's project deadlines at the end of each week to assess whether any changes are needed. If certain tasks are taking longer than expected, updating the timeline can relieve pressure and help avoid burnout. Doesn't this kind of review make it easier to adjust to new developments?

Balancing Ambition with Feasibility

Setting realistic deadlines is all about balancing ambition with feasibility. Have you ever tried to achieve something ambitious, only to feel paralyzed by the enormity of the task? Instead of setting one large deadline, break down your workload into smaller, more manageable milestones. For example, if you're launching a new product, setting deadlines for research, development, and marketing in separate stages can make the overall goal less daunting. Each smaller deadline allows you to focus on one task at a time, without feeling overwhelmed.

Incorporating buffer time into your schedule can also reduce anxiety and improve the quality of your work. Have you ever felt rushed to meet a deadline, only to wish you had more time? Buffer time allows for any delays, ensuring that your main deadline isn't affected. For instance, when planning an event, building in extra days for tasks like venue selection or logistics gives you the cushion you need to avoid last-minute stress.

Public commitments can also play a major role in staying on track. When you share your goals with others, you create external accountability that helps you stick to your timeline. For example, if you share a fitness goal with a friend or trainer, won't their regular check-ins help keep you focused? Similarly, informing colleagues or mentors about your work deadlines provides encouragement and keeps you accountable.

Finally, regularly reviewing your deadlines keeps your workflow adaptable. Wouldn't it be helpful to reassess your priorities weekly? This ongoing assessment ensures your deadlines stay relevant and realistic, especially in fast-paced environments. For example, a marketing team preparing for a product launch might set a SMART deadline to complete market research in two weeks, followed by three weeks for strategy development. Adding buffer time, such as an additional week for revisions, can reduce stress and improve the final product. Sharing this timeline with the entire team creates a sense of joint responsibility, and regular check-ins ensure the timeline stays on track.

Utilizing Motivational Tools

To effectively overcome procrastination, professionals need practical tools and techniques that boost motivation and keep them on task. This section explores several strategies that can help combat procrastination and promote productivity.

Vision boards are powerful visual tools that represent personal goals and aspirations. Have you ever tried collecting images, quotes, and affirmations that symbolize your desired achievements? Keeping a vision board in your workspace serves as a daily reminder of what you want to accomplish. For example, an entrepreneur might display visuals of successful companies or inspiring quotes to guide their journey. Wouldn't this constant visual encouragement help bridge the gap between your daily efforts and long-term success?

Another captivating method to stay productive is gamifying tasks. Have you ever added an element of fun to your responsibilities? By creating a points system where completing tasks earns rewards, you can turn work into a game. This approach not only makes tasks more enjoyable but also cultivates a sense of accomplishment. Could rewarding yourself for meeting goals keep you engaged and motivated?

Positive affirmations are another powerful tool against procrastination. Regularly repeating supportive statements can help counter negative thoughts and build confidence. Do you ever tell yourself, "I am capable" or "I manage my time well"? Incorporating affirmations like these into your daily routine can enhance motivation and resilience, especially during challenging moments.

Celebrating small wins is crucial for reinforcing positive behavior. Have you ever rewarded yourself for completing a small task? Acknowledging progress, no matter how minor, strengthens the habits that lead to success. Whether it's treating yourself after finishing a report or taking a break after a productive session, doesn't celebrating small victories make reaching larger goals more attainable?

Creating a supportive environment is another key factor in maintaining motivation. Surrounding yourself with encouraging people can significantly boost productivity. Engaging with like-minded peers through professional groups or online communities can provide the accountability and support you need. Would joining a mastermind group or an accountability circle help keep you on track with your goals?

An accountability partner is an effective strategy for staying focused. Have you ever worked with someone who shares similar goals? Regularly scheduled check-ins with a partner to discuss progress and challenges ensure consistency. For example, two colleagues aiming for career development could meet weekly to review their achievements and plan their next steps. Would the mutual support help you maintain momentum?

Joining goal-oriented groups can add another layer of motivation. Whether through online forums or local meetups, these communities allow you to share experiences and gain insights from others pursuing similar goals. Participating in discussions and collaborating on projects can help maintain your focus and productivity.

Seeking feedback is essential for growth. Constructive criticism from mentors, peers, or supervisors can provide valuable guidance. Have you ever asked for feedback on your progress? Regularly seeking input helps you identify areas for improvement while celebrating your strengths. For example, performance reviews can highlight achievements and direct your focus toward areas needing attention.

Establishing accountability rituals, such as regular progress reviews, helps ensure that your goals remain in focus. Do you set aside time to review your progress? Whether it's a monthly check-in with a mentor or a quarterly self-assessment, regularly evaluating your achievements promotes consistent effort. Entrepreneurs, for example, might create a framework for tracking business growth and reviewing their finances and marketing plans. Would a routine like this help keep you aligned with your goals?

Breaking tasks into manageable chunks is a powerful strategy against procrastination. This chapter has highlighted practical methods such as the 2-Minute Rule, task segmentation, bullet journaling, and time limits to effectively manage larger projects. Have you found that these strategies help clear mental clutter and keep you focused? For entrepreneurs juggling multiple responsibilities, these techniques offer efficient ways to handle workloads and consistently achieve milestones.

Embedding these motivational tools into your daily routine empowers you to maximize your potential and push both personal and professional success. Regular evaluation and adjustment of these strategies ensure their continued relevance. Wouldn't maintaining flexibility and continuously improving your approach help you stay productive and overcome procrastination? By mastering the skill of dividing tasks into manageable steps, you can transform overwhelming workloads into achievable objectives, fostering a sense of control and accomplishment on your journey.

References

20 Science-Based Hacks for Motivation | Expert Tips. (2020, January 5). Dr. Michelle Rozen - the Change Doctor. https://www.drmichellerozen.com/motivation/20-science-based-hacks/

FasterCapital. (n.d.). Setting deadlines and timelines for goal achievement. Retrieved from https://fastercapital.com/topics/setting-deadlines-and-timelines-for-goal-achievement.html

How To Use Positive Affirmations And Visualization Techniques To Boost Your Confidence And Motivation. (n.d.). FasterCapital. https://fastercapital.com/topics/how-to-use-positive-affirmations-and-visualization-techniques-to-boost-your-confidence-and-motivation.html

Lark Editorial Team. (2023, December 17). 2-Minute Rule: A Game-Changer for Productivity. Larksuite.com. https://www.larksuite.com/en_us/topics/productivity-glossary/2-minute-rule

Perry, E. (2022, September 21). What Is the 2-Minute Rule? Avoid Procrastination Quickly. Www.betterup.com. https://www.betterup.com/blog/what-is-the-two-minute-rule

Why Goal Setting is Important. (2023, April 17). Www.mikevestil.com. https://www.mikevestil.com/guides/why-goal-setting-is-important/

ENHANCING FOCUS AND CONCENTRATION

—————— • ★ • ——————

Focusing and concentrating on work is crucial for getting things done, especially when surrounded by distractions. Many professionals struggle to maintain attention during their busy days, but by setting up a workspace that supports deep focus, productivity and work performance can improve. This section will explore methods to enhance focus and reduce distractions, paving the way for better results.

To start, simple changes in the work environment can encourage focus. Improving factors like lighting, workspace setup, furniture comfort, and adding plants can create an inviting area that makes it easier to concentrate for longer periods. These practical adjustments can help reduce procrastination by creating a workspace conducive to focus and reducing distractions.

Creating an Ideal Work Environment

Creating a well-organized and comfortable workspace is crucial for maintaining focus and productivity. An effective environment can positively impact how well you work and how you feel throughout the day. This section explores how light and ambiance influence focus, the benefits of an organized space, the importance of comfortable furniture, and the soothing effects of greenery.

Lighting plays a significant role in focus and productivity. How well-lit a room is can directly affect your mindset and concentration. Natural light, in particular, can lift your mood and boost energy. If your workspace has windows, try positioning your desk near them to maximize natural light, which can significantly enhance both mood and productivity. On the other hand, poor lighting, especially when it's too dim, can make you feel tired and lose focus. Make sure your workspace has adequate lighting, combining general overhead lighting with task lighting, like desk lamps, to reduce eye strain and create an optimal work area.

Ambiance is another factor to consider when personalizing your space. What type of environment helps you concentrate best? Some people work well with soft background music, while others need complete silence. Experiment with color schemes, scents, or even adjusting the temperature to find the ambiance that supports your focus and helps prevent procrastination.

Organization is key to reducing distractions. A cluttered desk can make it difficult to concentrate. Decluttering and keeping only essential items close by can help you stay focused. Using drawers, shelves, or organizers can store non-essential items while keeping them accessible when needed. Creating specific zones in your workspace for different tasks can also help, such as separate areas for administrative tasks and creative work. This organization not only reduces procrastination but also allows for smoother transitions between tasks.

Comfortable furniture is essential for long-term productivity. Ergonomic furniture, such as a chair with proper back support and adjustable features, can reduce discomfort during extended periods of work. A chair that allows you to sit with your feet flat and your elbows at a right angle can help prevent physical strain, which can otherwise distract you from focusing on your tasks.

An adjustable desk is another worthwhile investment. Being able to switch between sitting and standing throughout the day helps maintain comfort and energy levels, which is important for staying focused and productive. This flexibility can help you avoid the fatigue that often leads to procrastination.

Finally, incorporating plants into your workspace can create a more relaxing and engaging environment. Plants not only improve the air quality but also help reduce stress, which can enhance focus and productivity. The concept of biophilic design, which integrates natural elements into workspaces, has become increasingly popular. Whether it's adding potted plants or using images of nature, these elements can help create a calming, productive workspace.

Using Time-Blocking Techniques

Time-blocking is a practical technique for managing focus and productivity by setting specific times to work on tasks. It's particularly useful in busy work environments filled with distractions. Instead of letting work spill into every part of the day, time-blocking provides a structured approach to organizing work hours.

Defining specific time blocks means assigning set times to focus on particular tasks. By doing this, you can better manage workloads and combat procrastination. For example, designating an hour in the morning for critical tasks creates a sense of urgency that helps you concentrate. Knowing you've scheduled time later for other tasks allows for deeper immersion in your current work. Tailoring these blocks to match your energy levels can make a significant difference; some people are more productive in the morning, while others may find afternoons or evenings to be their peak times.

Including breaks within your time-blocking plan is also crucial. Taking short breaks after intense work periods helps recharge your mind and maintain concentration over time. The Pomodoro Technique, which involves working for 25 minutes followed by a 5-minute break, is a popular method for keeping your mind fresh. Planned breaks prevent distractions by being intentional and regularly timed. Plus, effective breaks can spark creativity and enhance problem-solving when you return to work.

It's essential to adapt your time blocks based on the tasks you're handling. Different tasks may require varying levels of focus or time. For instance, complex projects may need longer blocks of uninterrupted time, while quicker tasks can fit into shorter chunks. Balancing intensive work with lighter tasks throughout the day helps maintain a steady level of concentration and prevents burnout.

Reflecting on your performance after completing time blocks can reveal patterns that improve your workflow. Keeping track of your accomplishments during each period can help identify your most productive times and allow you to adjust your schedule accordingly. For example, if you notice that you finish tasks more quickly in the late morning, you can prioritize challenging work during that time and save lighter tasks for later.

Time-blocking also helps manage distractions more effectively. In an age where notifications constantly interrupt us, adhering to a time-blocking schedule allows you to silence distractions during focus periods. Simply turning off email alerts or notifications during work blocks can greatly reduce interruptions and improve concentration.

This technique encourages a more planned approach to managing tasks. Instead of reacting to tasks as they come, organizing your day by assigning specific times to essential activities creates a proactive structure. This organized method reduces feelings of overwhelm. For example, a business owner can plan their day around client meetings, marketing efforts, financial tasks, and team management, ensuring each area has dedicated time without feeling rushed.

Incorporating personal time into your time blocks is equally important. Scheduling time for exercise, family, or personal hobbies helps maintain a balanced lifestyle. Knowing you've set aside time for personal priorities can enhance focus during work, as you won't feel guilty about neglecting personal needs. For instance, a planned break for a walk could recharge your mind and improve productivity for the rest of the day.

Consistency with time-blocking is key. Building this habit enhances focus over time by fostering a routine that naturally increases efficiency and concentration. Professionals who regularly use time-blocking techniques often feel more in control of their tasks, helping them successfully balance both their professional and personal lives.

Practicing Mindfulness and Meditation

Mindfulness offers a clear pathway to improved focus and reduced distractions. When you learn to be fully present, it becomes easier to stay engaged and keep wandering thoughts at bay. This heightened awareness not only enhances concentration but also helps manage emotions. Incorporating mindfulness practices into daily routines is simple and can blend well with busy schedules.

Meditation is particularly effective for sharpening focus. Regular meditation sessions improve cognitive functioning by teaching the mind to respond rather than react to external pressures. Studies show measurable improvements in attention span from these practices. Even basic meditation techniques, like deep breathing, provide significant benefits without requiring a large time commitment.

Taking mindful breaks during the workday can lead to noticeable improvements in productivity. These breaks refresh and reset your mind, preventing burnout. Instead of viewing breaks as interruptions, consider them moments to recharge your focus. Practicing grounding techniques before diving into work prepares you mentally and increases efficiency.

Establishing a culture of mindfulness can also benefit teams and organizations. Creating an environment where mindfulness is valued enhances communication and collaboration. Mindfulness practices foster a sense of community, where individuals support one another, promoting focus and productivity.

Understanding mindfulness begins with awareness of the present moment. Strengthening this awareness can significantly reduce distractions. Mindfulness can be practiced through simple activities, such as eating or walking mindfully, focusing on sensations like flavors, textures, or steps. These small practices require little effort but can lead to meaningful gains in focus and emotional balance.

Daily meditation is the foundation for deepening mindfulness. It doesn't need to be elaborate—even short periods of deep breathing can yield positive results. For instance, taking a few moments to focus on each breath can help ground you, improving focus over time and fostering a more centered mindset.

Incorporating mindful breaks throughout the workday can lead to productivity gains. Instead of reaching for snacks or mindlessly scrolling during breaks, try taking a few minutes to close your eyes and breathe deeply. These moments help reset your mental state, preparing you for the next task with a fresh perspective.

Fostering mindfulness in the workplace extends its benefits beyond individuals—it creates a supportive team atmosphere. Mindfulness can be incorporated into daily activities, like starting meetings with a brief exercise to help everyone focus. This practice encourages presence and builds connections among team members. Workplaces that promote mindfulness see reduced stress levels and increased employee satisfaction.

Organizations can support mindfulness by offering training or workshops focused on mindfulness techniques. These sessions might cover anything from basic practices to advanced guided meditations. Sharing personal experiences in these settings strengthens bonds within teams, promoting a supportive environment. Rituals like starting each workday with a moment of silence can create a positive atmosphere for the day ahead.

Mindfulness doesn't need to be limited to formal practices. It can be seamlessly integrated into daily life. For example, taking a moment to breathe deeply before responding to emails or during meetings can lead to more intentional communication. These mindful pauses provide clarity and improve focus, helping you manage distractions more effectively.

Incorporating simple mindfulness practices into your routine doesn't require drastic changes. Start small, with morning meditation or regular reminders to pause and breathe throughout the day. Over time, these practices can become part of your lifestyle, boosting focus and helping you manage distractions more effectively.

Workplaces that embrace mindfulness create a healthier, more productive environment. By prioritizing mindfulness, organizations demonstrate their commitment to employee well-being, leading to a more motivated and resilient workforce capable of handling fast-paced challenges with ease.

References

https://www.personatalent.com/development/how-to-improve-focus-and-concentration-in-the-workplace/

https://zealux.com/10-skills-to-improve-focus-and-concentration/

https://www.personatalent.com/productivity/executive-focus-how-to-avoid-distractions/

https://blog.ulliance.com/stay-focused-minimize-workplace-distractions

https://www.linkedin.com/pulse/strategies-avoid-distractions-workplace-proffice-tech-bi9xc

https://www.retainr.io/blog/how-to-maintain-focus-and-concentration-in-freelancing

EFFECTIVE TIME MANAGEMENT

———————— • ★ • ————————

E ffective time management is essential for boosting productivity and achieving professional goals. Managing your time well can mean the difference between feeling overwhelmed by a heavy workload and having an organized, balanced schedule. For professionals, entrepreneurs, and small business owners, mastering time management involves strategically prioritizing tasks to maximize efficiency and success.

This chapter explores various strategies to help you manage your time more effectively. You'll learn about tools like the Eisenhower Matrix, which helps you decide which tasks are urgent and important, and the ABC Method, used for ranking tasks by

their significance. You'll also discover techniques such as task batching, which reduces mental fatigue, and the importance of setting daily goals to maintain focus. By incorporating these methods, you can transform your approach to time management, resulting in increased productivity and reduced stress.

Prioritizing Tasks Effectively

Understanding how to prioritize tasks is key to boosting efficiency in your daily routines. One of the most effective methods is the Eisenhower Matrix, a tool that helps distinguish between urgent tasks that need immediate attention and important tasks that contribute to long-term goals. For example, responding to an urgent client email is pressing, while planning for next quarter's business goals is important but not immediate. By categorizing tasks into one of four groups—Do, Schedule, Delegate, and Delete—you can quickly determine what needs attention now, what can be planned for, what can be delegated, and what can be eliminated.

To get started, list your tasks and categorize them. Tasks that are both urgent and important belong in the 'Do' category and require immediate action. Important but non-urgent tasks should be placed in the 'Schedule' category, where you set a time to handle them. Urgent but less important tasks go into the 'Delegate' category—they can be handed off to someone else. Finally, tasks that are neither urgent nor important fall into the 'Delete' category and can be eliminated. The Eisenhower Matrix helps you focus on what truly matters, reducing stress and boosting productivity.

Another useful prioritization method is the ABC Method, where tasks are ranked based on priority: 'A' for the highest priority, 'B' for medium priority, and 'C' for the lowest. Begin your day by listing all tasks and assigning 'A' to the most critical ones—these should be tackled first. 'B' tasks are important but can wait, while 'C' tasks are minor and can be done if time permits. Systematically working through 'A' tasks before 'B' and 'C' ensures that the most essential work gets priority, improving your overall effectiveness.

For example, if you have a project report due on Friday, that would be labeled as 'A.' On the other hand, answering non-urgent emails might be a 'B,' and cleaning your desk could fall under 'C.' Labeling tasks this way allows you to focus on what's most important when needed.

Another key strategy is task batching. Grouping similar tasks together helps reduce mental fatigue and allows for longer periods of focused work. For example, instead of sporadically checking emails throughout the day, you can schedule specific time slots dedicated to handling them. Likewise, scheduling blocks of time for meetings, phone calls, or creative work lets you immerse yourself in each task without interruptions. This approach enhances concentration and drives efficiency.

Think about your routine—if you handle multiple financial reports, batch them together rather than spreading them out across the week. Similarly, setting aside time to handle all phone calls at once helps prevent scattered interruptions throughout your day. This focused method allows for greater concentration and efficiency.

Setting daily goals is another practical time management tool. By identifying three to five main tasks to complete each day, you create clear, attainable objectives. Daily goals provide direction and offer a sense of accomplishment as you check off completed tasks.

At the start of each day, take a few moments to outline what you aim to achieve by day's end. For example, your goals might include submitting a project proposal, meeting with a client, and sending a follow-up email. Having clear goals eliminates uncertainty and gives you a roadmap for the day. Completing tasks provides immediate feedback on your progress, which is both rewarding and motivating.

The common goal of these techniques is to optimize how you spend your time. They help professionals and entrepreneurs face daily distractions and prioritize their work effectively. Whether you use the Eisenhower Matrix for structure, the ABC Method for prioritization, task batching for focused work, or daily goals for clear objectives, each technique offers a way to enhance productivity while reducing stress.

In practice, the Eisenhower Matrix might reveal that many of your daily interruptions are urgent but unnecessary for your long-term goals. Delegating these tasks can free up valuable time for more productive work. The ABC Method ensures that your energy is directed toward essential tasks, leading to meaningful accomplishments in your career.

Task batching supports this by giving you uninterrupted time to focus on complex jobs, helping you maintain concentration and quality of work. Meanwhile, setting daily goals ensures that your energy is directed toward what matters most, allowing you to track progress and stay motivated.

By incorporating these techniques into your routines, you establish a solid framework for time management. This shift moves you from a reactive mindset to a proactive strategy for handling your workload. The result? Enhanced productivity and a more balanced, satisfying professional life.

Utilizing Productivity Tools and Apps

To maximize your time and boost productivity, using the right productivity tools and apps is essential. These tools streamline tasks and provide a structured approach to managing your time effectively.

A key category of these tools is task management software. Programs like Trello and Asana are excellent for visually tracking projects and collaborating with teams. They use boards, lists, and cards to help you instantly see what needs to be done. For instance, Trello allows you to use boards divided into columns that represent different stages of a project, such as "To Do," "In Progress," and "Done." Moving tasks between these columns offers a clear view of your progress. Asana, on the other hand, focuses on creating tasks within projects and assigning responsibilities along with due dates, ensuring that everyone knows what they need to do.

To fully leverage task management software, familiarize yourself with its features. Start by creating boards or projects that reflect your actual workflow. Break larger objectives into smaller, manageable tasks. Regularly update the status of tasks to keep communication clear and reduce confusion.

Time tracking apps are also invaluable for monitoring daily activities. Tools like Toggl and RescueTime help you see where your time is going. For instance, Toggl allows you to start a timer for a task and stop it when you're done, providing an accurate account of how long you spend on each activity. RescueTime runs in the background and automatically tracks time spent on different applications and websites, categorizing activities as productive or distracting. This insight can help you minimize interruptions and focus on important work.

To use time tracking apps effectively, track everything you do for a week without altering your habits. This will give you a baseline for identifying areas of improvement. Afterward, set goals like reducing time on social media or increasing focus on high-priority tasks. Review your reports regularly to monitor changes in your productivity habits.

Calendar applications are another staple for effective time management. Tools like Google Calendar and Outlook allow you to schedule tasks and meetings efficiently. Google Calendar offers features like color-coding events, setting recurring alerts, and integrating with Google Meet for seamless meeting setups. Outlook provides similar functionality with strong integration into other Microsoft tools. Using these calendar apps lets you organize your day, week, or month in advance, making it easier to allocate time for specific tasks and avoid scheduling conflicts.

To maximize calendar apps, try time blocking—a method of dividing your day into blocks dedicated to specific tasks or activities. Schedule high-priority work during your most productive hours, and don't forget to include breaks to help you recharge. Regularly review and adjust your calendar to ensure it aligns with your evolving priorities.

Note-taking software is also an essential part of any productivity toolkit. Programs like Evernote and Notion help you organize information, ideas, and project notes. Evernote allows you to create notebooks, tag content for easy access, and even scan paper documents using your phone, making it ideal for organizing and storing important information. Notion combines note-taking with project management, enabling users to create databases, wikis, and kanban boards all in one place.

To make the most of note-taking software, create a structure that suits your work. Use notebooks or pages for different areas of your professional and personal life. Tags can help you quickly find relevant notes, and regular reviews will keep your workspace organized and up to date.

BALANCING WORK AND REST

— • ★ • —

Finding a balance between work and rest is essential to avoiding burnout and maintaining long-term productivity. One of the first steps toward achieving this balance is understanding what work-life balance truly means. It involves creating clear boundaries between work and personal time to support mental health and maintain motivation. This can be as simple as setting specific work hours and ensuring they don't overlap with personal time. By keeping work and leisure distinct, you allow yourself to recharge, which enhances both productivity and job satisfaction.

Incorporating downtime into your daily routine is crucial for boosting both productivity and creativity. Taking breaks during work hours gives your brain a chance to relax and recover, leading to better decision-making and problem-solving abilities. For instance, scheduling brief breaks every hour and a longer break at lunch can significantly improve focus and efficiency. Planning vacations or days off in advance is equally important to ensure you have adequate rest, which helps prevent chronic fatigue.

Engaging in self-care is another effective way to maintain a healthy work-life balance. Activities like mindfulness, meditation, and regular exercise positively affect both emotional and physical well-being. Mindfulness can help alleviate stress, creating a calm state of mind, particularly in demanding work environments. Regular exercise not only boosts physical health but also reduces symptoms of anxiety and depression, improving overall mental well-being. Including these activities in your routine fosters resilience and promotes a positive outlook on both work and personal life.

Listening to your body is key to preventing overexertion and ensuring you work efficiently. Pay attention to signals such as fatigue or stress, which can guide you to take necessary breaks. Understanding your energy levels allows you to schedule demanding tasks during peak performance times and reserve less critical tasks for when you're feeling less energetic. This self-awareness helps you manage your workload more sustainably, reducing the risk of burnout and enhancing productivity.

References

https://www.usa.edu/blog/time-management-techniques/

https://asana.com/resources/eisenhower-matrix

https://thebusinessdive.com/time-management-strategies

https://www.linkedin.com/pulse/maximizing-productivity-femmeforceco-qb7ae?trk=organization_guest_main-feed-card_feed-article-content

https://www.pinktum.com/en/blog/methoden-und-techniken-fuer-ein-perfektes-zeitmanagement/

https://www.coursesidekick.com/management/3898683

GOAL SETTING FOR SUCCESS

— ★ —

G oal setting is essential for anyone looking to succeed, whether in their personal life or career. It provides a clear path to achieving objectives and helps keep you motivated. In today's busy work environments, where distractions are everywhere, having practical methods for setting goals is crucial. This keeps professionals focused and ensures they are on the right track to achieving what truly matters to them. This section explores tips and strategies for effective goal setting and how to align your objectives with your core values.

One of the most reliable ways to set goals is through the SMART Goals Framework. This framework breaks goal setting into five clear categories: Specific, Measurable, Achievable, Relevant, and Time-Bound. By using this framework, you can create concrete goals that are easy to understand and act upon. For example, instead of saying, "I want to improve my sales," you might say, "I want to increase my monthly sales by 20% through targeted marketing campaigns and more effective customer engagement." This specificity forms a clear picture of what success will look like.

Specific goals not only provide clarity but also enhance motivation. When you know exactly what you want to achieve, it becomes easier to create a plan to reach that goal. This clarity also boosts teamwork, as everyone understands the goal and can work toward it collectively. When everyone is on the same page, it leads to greater efficiency and improved morale.

The next component, measurable goals, is fundamental for tracking progress. Establishing criteria and metrics for success allows you to assess how well you're doing. For instance, tracking new customer acquisition or repeat orders can shed light on the effectiveness of your sales strategy. Having measurable goals also keeps you accountable. Celebrating small wins when you reach certain benchmarks keeps motivation alive and provides a sense of accomplishment.

Achievable goals focus on setting realistic targets. It's vital to ensure your goals are feasible to avoid frustration or discouragement. Thoughtfully assessing the resources at your disposal, time constraints, and potential challenges helps you set realistic objectives. For example, if you're launching a new product, assess your budget and production capabilities. A more achievable goal might be to launch a prototype first, gathering feedback before a full-scale release. This approach reduces pressure and keeps the focus on manageable steps.

Next, relevant goals ensure that what you're striving for aligns with your values and what's important in your life. When your goals reflect your core values, you're more driven to achieve them. For example, if family time is a high priority, setting a goal to improve your time management skills to create better work-life balance becomes much easier to commit to.

When your objectives are in sync with your personal values, you're investing your time and energy more meaningfully. This sense of alignment fosters ownership and encourages you to take the necessary steps to reach your goals.

Aligning Personal Values with Goals

Connecting your goals to your personal values leads to increased motivation and commitment. Your core values act as a guide for your actions and decisions, making it essential to understand what truly matters to you. To identify your values, begin with self-reflection. Think about moments when you felt genuinely happy and fulfilled. What key aspects of your life were present during those times?

Creating a list can also help. Consider categories like family, career, personal growth, or health, and jot down words or phrases that resonate with you. Then, prioritize these values by identifying which ones you can't compromise on. Another useful technique is mind mapping—write "Core Values" in the center of a page and branch out to related values. This visual method can clarify what's most important to you.

The next step is to integrate your core values with your goals. Review your current goals and check if they align with your values. If not, adjust them to better reflect what you truly believe in. For example, if health is one of your core values, you could set specific goals around healthier eating or regular exercise. Aligning your goals with your values adds a deeper sense of purpose, motivating you to stay committed and make consistent efforts.

Since values can evolve over time, it's important to periodically evaluate your goals against your values. Set aside time every few months to revisit your goals and assess their relevance. As life changes, so can your priorities. Keeping a journal to track your progress and thoughts can provide valuable insights and help you spot patterns that may require adjustments. This adaptability ensures that your goals remain relevant to your current life.

There are numerous examples of success that come from aligning goals with personal values. Take Sarah, for instance—an entrepreneur whose core value is creativity. She founded a tech company focused on innovative solutions and found immense satisfaction in her work because it aligned with her passion. Similarly, John, who values environmental sustainability, proposed a green initiative at his company, enhancing both his role and his connection to a cause he deeply cares about.

Then there's Maria, a healthcare worker who values compassion. Her dedication to improving patient care led her to implement a more patient-centered approach at her hospital. These examples highlight the profound motivation that comes from aligning goals with core values, leading to success in both personal and professional arenas.

Short-Term vs. Long-Term Goal Setting

Understanding the difference between short-term and long-term goals is crucial for successful achievement. Short-term goals are generally those you aim to accomplish in a few months or less. These straightforward objectives help you make progress toward larger aspirations. For example, completing a project report by the end of the week or improving your daily work efficiency by 10% over the next month would fall into this category. Short-term goals boost morale and provide essential stepping stones toward bigger visions.

In contrast, long-term goals are broader objectives that span a more extended timeframe, typically years. These goals help define the overall direction of your pursuits. For instance, an entrepreneur might aim to expand their business internationally over the next five years, while someone else might plan to reach a senior position in their field within a decade. Long-term goals provide vision and purpose, motivating you to keep striving even when challenges arise.

Maintaining a balance between short-term and long-term goals is key. A practical technique is breaking long-term goals into smaller, manageable short-term milestones. This approach makes the larger vision easier to tackle. For example, if your long-term goal is to write a book within two years, you could set short-term milestones like outlining chapters in a month, writing a specific number of words each day, or completing the first draft in six months. Celebrating these smaller achievements keeps your motivation high and your progress on track.

Using goal-tracking tools can make a significant difference in maintaining a clear view of what you want to achieve. Digital project management tools like Trello or Asana help visually organize your tasks and hold you accountable. Productivity apps can also turn goal-setting into a fun and rewarding experience.

Keeping a journal where you write down your goals and update your progress is another effective option. This tangible record reinforces motivation, showcasing what you've accomplished while highlighting areas that may need more attention. A vision board can also be an effective strategy, offering a daily visual reminder of what you're striving for and making your goals feel more tangible.

Embracing technology can further assist in managing goals. Setting reminders on calendars or utilizing notifications helps keep you focused on your objectives. With consistent tracking, you can adjust your strategies as needed, ensuring your goals remain achievable and relevant.

This comprehensive approach to setting and tracking both short-term and long-term goals increases the likelihood of success while helping you maintain a balanced and fulfilling life.

References

Aligning Personal Values: The Value of Cultural Fit in Company Values - Galt. (2023, December 20). Galt. https://galtstaffing.com/2023/12/20/aligning-personal-values-the-value-of-cultural-fit-in-company-values/

Boogaard, K. (2023, December 26). How to write SMART goals. Atlassian. https://www.atlassian.com/blog/productivity/how-to-write-smart-goals

Cruz, L. (2021, July 20). Short Term vs Long Term Goals (Examples, FAQs). ClickUp Blog. https://clickup.com/blog/short-term-vs-long-term-goals/

Mind Tools Content Team. (2023). SMART goals. Mind Tools; Mind Tools. https://www.mindtools.com/a4wo118/smart-goals

Pervaiz, S., Li, G., & He, Q. (2021, December 15). The Mechanism of goal-setting Participation's Impact on Employees' Proactive behavior, Moderated Mediation Role of Power Distance (Y. Bilan, Ed.). PLOS ONE; NCBI. https://doi.org/10.1371/journal.pone.0260625

Price, N. (2019, January 4). The Difference Between Short-Term and Long-Term Goal Planning | BoardEffect. BoardEffect. https://www.boardeffect.com/blog/difference-short-term-long-term-goal-planning/

MAINTAINING ACCOUNTABILITY

———— • ★ • ————

Maintaining accountability is essential for achieving goals, whether you're a professional or an entrepreneur. In a world full of distractions, accountability systems help keep you focused and motivated. It's not just about self-discipline; it's about creating structures that encourage ongoing effort and commitment to your objectives.

A key part of this is finding an accountability partner—someone reliable, honest, and committed to growth. Regular check-ins with this partner allow you to assess progress, make adjustments, and celebrate small wins. These meetings help you stay on track and keep your goals in focus.

Overcoming common challenges, like scheduling conflicts or mismatched partnerships, is also important. Choose a partner who aligns with your working style and set clear expectations for communication and support.

By integrating accountability into your routine, you're more likely to stay committed and achieve your goals, no matter the obstacles.

Finding an Accountability Partner

Accountability partners play a crucial role for professionals and entrepreneurs. In busy work environments where distractions are common, having someone to support your goals can make a significant difference. An accountability partner helps reinforce your commitments and provides encouragement, whether you're aiming for business success or personal improvement.

An effective partnership is based on mutual support. Both partners motivate each other, keeping discipline intact even when distractions arise. For example, if your goal is to focus on business development instead of social media, your partner can track your progress and remind you to stay on task. Accountability software can further enhance this dynamic by monitoring activities and generating reports, ensuring both partners stay informed and motivated.

Choosing the right accountability partner is key. Ideally, select someone with similar interests and goals. This shared foundation makes it easier to support each other. Your partner could be a family member, friend, coworker, or coach. Look for key traits such as trustworthiness, motivation, and a genuine interest in your success. Comfort in sharing challenges and receiving feedback is also essential.

Once you've found a partner, create a clear plan of action. Set specific, measurable goals using the SMART framework—Specific, Measurable, Achievable, Relevant, and Time-bound. This keeps both partners focused. Agree on a regular schedule to check in, share insights, and offer feedback. Consistent updates are critical for maintaining accountability and staying on track.

Before each meeting, prepare tasks that are challenging yet realistic. Choose a communication method that works for both partners, whether it's quick texts, phone calls, or face-to-face meetings. Keeping communication lines open is key to a successful partnership.

The benefits of having an accountability partner go beyond reaching goals. These partnerships can enhance social skills, foster responsibility, and build empathy. Knowing someone is counting on you to meet commitments underlines the importance of reliability. This dynamic can even lead to lasting friendships and a stronger sense of community.

However, challenges do arise. One common issue is finding a compatible partner. Understanding each other's work style and communication preferences is crucial. A trial period can help determine if the partnership works well long-term. If it doesn't, don't hesitate to seek another partner better suited to your needs.

Scheduling conflicts can also be a problem. To avoid this, establish regular times to connect and adjust your calendars accordingly. Predictable check-ins help maintain accountability and commitment to achieving goals.

An additional value of accountability partnerships lies in the insights and feedback they provide. Sharing strategies and resources can help combat procrastination and offer new learning opportunities. This collaborative approach simplifies the path to success, while mutual support during tough times makes obstacles feel less daunting.

It's important to establish a systematic strategy for communication. Decide how often you'll check in and which methods to use, whether it's regular meetings, shared documents, or specific apps. Flexibility is equally important; be willing to adapt as circumstances evolve. Honest feedback and encouragement strengthen the partnership.

Finally, remember that accountability is a two-way street. Both partners must commit to supporting and celebrating each other's achievements. This shared effort creates a positive atmosphere that boosts the chances of success, helping both individuals reach their goals together.

REGULAR PROGRESS CHECK-INS

———————— • ★ • ————————

Regular evaluations are essential for maintaining accountability and reaching goals. They serve as checkpoints, allowing individuals to assess progress, pinpoint areas for improvement, and make adjustments as needed. Incorporating these evaluations into your goal-setting routine can boost productivity and keep you aligned with your objectives.

One of the primary benefits of regular evaluations is establishing clear expectations. Setting guidelines for how often to review progress creates a structured roadmap toward achieving your goals. For instance, organizing weekly or bi-weekly evaluations can help identify effective strategies and areas that need rethinking. Early assessments prevent small issues from becoming bigger problems, keeping you focused and driven.

Evaluations also help verify whether current objectives are still relevant. This involves checking if your goals align with broader personal or professional ambitions. Making sure your goals remain pertinent avoids wasting time on endeavors that no longer serve a purpose. For example, an entrepreneur who initially wants to expand a product line may need to shift priorities due to market changes. Regular evaluations can highlight when adjustments are needed based on new circumstances.

Creating time-based plans is another key element of effective evaluations. Breaking long-term goals into smaller, manageable tasks helps clarify what needs to be done and sets realistic deadlines. For example, if you plan to complete a major project in six months, segmenting it into monthly tasks makes it less overwhelming. Tracking progress against these smaller milestones allows for periodic reassessment and keeps the larger goal in sight.

Documentation plays a crucial role in the evaluation process. Keeping track of goals, tasks, milestones, and deadlines provides reference points for assessing progress. Tools like calendars, planners, or digital software help with efficient documentation. Visual aids, like checklists or progress bars, can enhance motivation and highlight areas needing more attention. For instance, a marketing team aiming to increase social media engagement by 20% over three months can document each step, such as creating content and monitoring metrics. Reviewing these actions during evaluations helps refine strategies and track effectiveness.

Routine evaluations also encourage the creation of action plans, outlining specific steps to achieve objectives. These plans should be both ambitious and feasible, typically evaluated on a weekly basis. For example, setting a goal to work out three times a week is more practical than simply aiming to "exercise more." Weekly evaluations offer immediate insights for adjustments and improvements.

Incorporating the SMART criteria—Specific, Measurable, Achievable, Relevant, and Time-bound—into your evaluations enhances their effectiveness. A vague goal like "improve sales" becomes more actionable when turned into a SMART goal, such as "increase monthly sales by 15% within six months through targeted online ads." Regular evaluations against these clear benchmarks help measure progress and ensure that goals remain attainable.

Evaluations also boost intrinsic motivation and self-efficacy. Knowing that progress will be reviewed regularly fosters a sense of accountability and drive. Goals that align with personal interests lead to higher levels of commitment. For instance, a business owner passionate about customer service might set a goal to improve client satisfaction. Regular check-ins can track improvements through customer feedback, offering a sense of fulfillment and motivating further efforts.

Consistency in evaluations helps prevent complacency and keeps efforts on track. Even when setbacks occur, check-ins provide a framework for adapting to challenges. For example, if a project falls behind due to unexpected changes, early identification through routine evaluations allows for immediate course corrections.

Finally, frequent evaluations promote a culture of continuous growth. Reflecting on progress cultivates a habit of critical self-assessment, fostering ongoing learning and adaptation. Whether refining business strategies or improving personal skills, the iterative process of evaluation ensures steady growth and goal achievement.

Rewarding Yourself for Achievements

Acknowledging and celebrating accomplishments plays an important role in maintaining motivation, particularly in professional settings. Despite the rush of modern workplaces, taking moments to appreciate achievements can significantly boost morale and engagement.

First and foremost, celebrating successes reinforces positive behavior. When individuals or teams meet challenging objectives, recognition brings validation to their hard work. This validation not only lifts spirits but also inspires continued high performance. When people feel appreciated for their efforts, they are more likely to maintain or even exceed their productivity.

Moreover, celebrations serve as strong reminders of past successes. In environments often focused on completing tasks, pausing to reflect on progress helps to highlight how much has been accomplished. This reflection is vital for long-term motivation, providing a sense of achievement. It can be encouraging to realize that once-daunting goals have transformed into milestones that have already been completed.

Celebrating accomplishments also allows individuals to solidify their learnings from the journey to achieving goals. Each project comes with its own challenges and lessons. By recognizing successes, professionals can discuss what strategies were effective and what adjustments might be required for future tasks. This reflective practice guarantees continuous improvement, both for an individual and within the team.

Additionally, acknowledgment and celebration can help strengthen relationships and create a positive workplace culture. Even simple celebratory events bring coworkers closer together. When team members celebrate each other's successes, it fosters a sense of community and shared values. Such relationships are key to creating a unified team working toward common objectives.

In terms of practical methods for celebrating success, various approaches can be effective. One way is through public recognition. Sharing achievements during team meetings or in company updates can help individuals feel valued and motivate others to perform. A monthly newsletter that highlights team achievements can efficiently keep everyone informed and inspired.

Another attractive method is to incorporate small, meaningful rewards. They don't need to be extravagant; even simple tokens or extra time off can effectively show appreciation. The key is personalizing the rewards to align with the preferences of the individual or team. For example, if a team completes a project ahead of schedule, treating them to a casual dress day or arranging a team lunch may express gratitude effectively.

Using technology can sometimes enhance celebrating achievements. Tools such as messaging apps or shared calendars can ensure that milestones are highlighted promptly. Collaborative platforms that visually track progress, like project management software, also provide opportunities to celebrate key achievements. Not only do these tools keep everyone updated, but they also help create a collective sense of accomplishment.

Many organizations often fall prey to the "on-to-the-next" mentality, which can contribute to burnout. This attitude encourages continuous progress without recognizing the importance of celebrating hard work. Shifting this perspective by integrating regular moments of acknowledgment into everyday workflow can sustain motivation and prevent exhaustion. Celebrating wins regularly helps the practice become part of the professional culture.

Moreover, celebrations shouldn't solely focus on major milestones. It's equally important to acknowledge smaller wins and incremental progress. Smaller celebrations provide immediate satisfaction and ongoing encouragement. For instance, recognizing a halfway milestone in a lengthy project can uplift spirits and keep motivation alive.

Final Thoughts

Accountability is a powerful tool for achieving goals. It promotes commitment and ensures continuous progress. With an accountability partner, professionals can effectively navigate distractions while remaining focused on their objectives. The collaboration between partners strengthens motivation and discipline, making the pursuit of goals both manageable and rewarding. Clear goal-setting, regular check-ins, and effective communication solidify this partnership, enhancing productivity significantly.

Finding the right accountability partner starts with seeking someone who shares your interests, helping to establish a strong support system. Ongoing evaluations and constructive feedback are key components of this relationship, fostering a culture of improvement and adaptability. Challenges such as coordinating schedules or finding a compatible partner may arise, but the benefits of enhanced social skills, a sense of personal responsibility, and community contribute to achieving success. Accountability partnerships not only assist in goal realization but also encourage personal growth and the formation of meaningful connections.

References

https://ca.indeed.com/career-advice/career-development/accountability-partner

https://www.linkedin.com/pulse/harnessing-power-accountability-partners-path-success-veroneau-ms-ajwcc

https://fastercapital.com/content/Goal-Setting--Accountability-Partners--Teaming-Up--The-Benefits-of-Accountability-Partners-in-Goal-Setting.html

https://www.linkedin.com/pulse/what-your-goals-need-accountability-partner-dewayne-griffin-cpcu

https://topresume.com/career-advice/tips-behind-the-art-of-being-an-accountability-partner

https://recreation.duke.edu/story/accountability-partners-dont-achieve-your-goals-alone/

SUSTAINING LONG-TERM PRODUCTIVITY

———— • ★ • ————

Sustaining long-term productivity is crucial for anyone aiming to keep growing and succeeding. In today's fast-paced work environment, distractions are everywhere, and maintaining motivation and efficiency can be challenging. To stay consistently productive over time, it's important to explore strategies and methods that professionals, entrepreneurs, and small business owners can use. These approaches are not just about doing more work; they focus on building a mindset that supports long-term progress while avoiding burnout.

This piece will explore foundational methods that help create lasting habits. Techniques like habit stacking and using commitment devices can turn actions into consistent behaviors. Tracking your progress is also essential, as it keeps you motivated and helps you enjoy the process of building productive habits. Practical examples and additional advice will show how to apply these strategies effectively, with a case study included to illustrate how integrating these methods can lead to significant productivity improvements.

The goal is to equip readers with actionable tools and knowledge to maintain long-term productivity in both their professional and personal lives.

Creating Sustainable Habits

Building habits that support consistent productivity is crucial for preventing procrastination and maintaining efficiency over time. This section explores techniques to help form productive habits and sustain a strong, long-term mindset.

Habit Stacking

Habit stacking is a simple yet powerful strategy for integrating new behaviors into your daily routine. It works by linking a new habit to an existing one, making it easier to maintain. When you connect a new behavior with something you already do, it becomes part of your familiar routine. For instance, if you habitually drink coffee each morning, you could stack a new habit, like reviewing your to-do list, right after your first sip. This strategy takes advantage of how easily your brain connects actions.

To use habit stacking, first identify a habit you always perform without fail. Then, think of a simple action you want to turn into a habit and link it to that existing routine. Keep the new behavior short and manageable to avoid feeling overwhelmed.

Setting Actions in Stone

Commitment devices are another effective tool for reinforcing new habits. These devices help you commit to a specific behavior by "locking in" future actions. By making clear commitments to yourself or others and using environmental cues, you increase accountability. For example, scheduling a workout with a friend creates a social commitment, making you less likely to skip it. Similarly, apps that restrict device usage during certain hours reduce distractions and improve focus.

To create effective commitment devices, consider making public commitments or setting automatic reminders. Choose tools that fit your lifestyle, ensuring they effectively reinforce your desired behaviors.

Tracking Progress

Tracking progress is essential for maintaining motivation and seeing improvements. Visual tools like charts, journals, or apps provide concrete proof of your efforts. These tools allow you to track daily accomplishments and identify areas for improvement. For example, using a simple chart to check off each day you follow a new habit builds a sense of achievement and consistency.

Find a tracking method that suits you, whether it's a digital app or a handwritten journal, and make it a habit to update it regularly. Periodically review your patterns to determine what's working and where adjustments are needed.

Emotional Reinforcement

Linking positive emotions to your productive habits is key to making them stick. When a habit feels enjoyable, you're more likely to continue it. You can achieve this by rewarding yourself or incorporating activities you enjoy. For example, listening to your favorite music while working can create a positive association with productivity, making the task more enjoyable. Over time, this strengthens your commitment to the habit.

To enhance enjoyment, explore ways to make your habits fun. Whether through small rewards, engaging activities, or positive self-talk, ensure the reinforcement feels genuine and contributes to your overall experience.

Practical Examples and Additional Tips

Here are some practical examples that illustrate these concepts. For habit stacking, if someone wants to read more, they might decide to read two pages of a book right after brushing their teeth at night. The familiar bedtime routine helps establish the new reading habit.

When it comes to setting actions in stone, you might declare your intention to prepare for a marathon publicly. Sharing this goal with friends and family adds social pressure and makes it more likely you will stick to your running schedule.

Tracking progress can be straightforward. You could keep a bullet journal where you log daily activities related to your new habit. Regularly reviewing this journal can give you insights into your progress and show you where you might need to improve, creating a clear path for continued growth.

Emotional reinforcement can be as simple as rewarding yourself with a piece of dark chocolate after completing an hour of focused work. By associating tasks with small treats, even daunting responsibilities can feel more manageable and enjoyable.

Case Study

Let's examine a case study to illustrate how these strategies can be applied. Sarah, a busy professional, wants to improve her fitness despite her packed schedule. She implements the following steps:

Stack Habits: Sarah links her habit of stretching to her morning tea routine, making it easier to incorporate into her day.

Set Actions in Stone: She books workout sessions with a friend, creating a social commitment that makes it harder to skip.

Track Progress: Sarah uses a fitness app to log her workouts, providing a visual representation of her progress and keeping her motivated.

Reinforce Emotionally: After completing a successful week of workouts, she rewards herself with a relaxing bath, associating exercise with relaxation and self-care.

By combining these strategies, Sarah seamlessly integrates her fitness goals into her daily life. This demonstrates the power of habit stacking, commitment devices, progress tracking, and emotional reinforcement in achieving sustainable productivity.

Continuously Evaluating and Adjusting Goals

Regularly reviewing and refining your goals is essential for sustaining long-term productivity. This practice ensures that your objectives remain relevant and continue to motivate personal and professional growth.

Regular Review Schedule

Developing a consistent schedule to assess your goals is crucial. Set aside specific times every few months to evaluate your progress, adjust for new priorities, and ensure that your goals align with your evolving aspirations. For example, busy professionals might find it helpful to dedicate time at the end of each quarter to reflect on accomplishments, recognize shifts in priorities, and modify goals as necessary. This habit keeps the focus on continuous improvement and maintains accountability for results.

SMART Adjustments

Once you establish a review routine, fine-tune your goals using the SMART criteria: Specific, Measurable, Achievable, Relevant, and Time-bound. SMART goals help maintain motivation by providing clear, measurable objectives. For instance, rather than a vague goal like "increase sales," specify a target such as "boost sales by 10% over the next quarter." This approach ensures your goals are both challenging and realistic, avoiding the frustration of setting unattainable objectives.

Seeking Feedback

Incorporating feedback from peers, mentors, or colleagues is another key element of refining your goals. Their insights can offer fresh perspectives and ideas you might not have considered. Feedback also adds accountability and encourages commitment. For example, if an entrepreneur is launching a new product, expert advice can help clarify market trends or potential challenges. Regular feedback sessions should be part of your review schedule to ensure you're on the right path.

Goal Expansion

As you make progress, revisit your goals to consider expanding them. Raising your aspirations over time can keep you motivated and foster a sense of continuous achievement. For instance, after reaching a significant milestone, like securing a major client, it's important to acknowledge the success and set new, more ambitious goals. This approach promotes ongoing improvement and a forward-thinking mindset.

Dealing with Setbacks Constructively

How you respond to setbacks is crucial for maintaining long-term productivity. Setbacks are inevitable, but viewing them through a constructive lens helps you bounce back and continue moving forward. By reframing obstacles as learning opportunities, employing recovery strategies, building a resilient mindset, and celebrating small adjustments, you can maintain momentum.

Reframing Setbacks

Reframing setbacks means changing how you perceive challenges. Instead of viewing them as failures, consider them valuable lessons. This perspective reduces their emotional impact and fosters a healthier outlook on failure. Asking yourself, "What can I learn from this experience?" encourages growth and improves your approach in the future.

Strategies for Recovery

Having a recovery plan is essential for getting back on track. Techniques like journaling or analyzing what went wrong can provide clarity on how to avoid similar pitfalls. Engaging in stress-reducing activities and discussing challenges with mentors can also rejuvenate your focus. After a setback, taking time for self-care and approaching your goals with renewed energy can make all the difference.

Building a Resilient Mindset

Developing a resilient mindset combines inspiration with practical techniques to strengthen mental toughness. Hearing stories of resilience from others can motivate you, showing how people have overcome obstacles. Practices like positive self-talk, visualization, and mindfulness help you stay grounded, even when facing difficulties.

Celebrating Adjustments

Recognizing progress, even after setbacks, is key to maintaining a positive outlook. Acknowledging small wins keeps morale high. For example, if a business owner faces repeated investor rejections, noting each improvement can boost confidence and highlight ongoing progress.

References

https://fastercapital.com/content/Effective-Habits--Personal-Development-Plans--Designing-Personal-Development-Plans-for-Effective-Habit-Formation.html

https://jamesclear.com/goals-systems

https://www.linkedin.com/pulse/master-habit-loop-productivity-success-devesh-sharma

https://bradsugars.com/high-performance-habits/

https://jamesclear.com/habit-tracker

https://hr.uiowa.edu/news/2022/01/make-lasting-change-stacking-good-habits

www.ingramcontent.com/pod-product-compliance
Lightning Source LLC
Chambersburg PA
CBHW040908210326
41597CB00029B/5015